BABE DIDRIKSON ZAHARIAS

MULTISPORT SUPERSTAR

JOE LEVIT

LERNER PUBLICATIONS ◆ MINNEAPOLIS

To my son, Druv. Always remember, you can do anything you set your mind to.

Lerner Publications Company
An imprint of Lerner Publishing Group, Inc.
241 First Avenue North
Minneapolis, MN 55401 USA

For reading levels and more information, look up this title at www.lernerbooks.com.

Main body text set in Myriad Pro Semibold.
Typeface provided by Adobe.

Editor: Shee Yang **Designer:** Susan Fienhage

Library of Congress Cataloging-in-Publication Data

Names: Levit, Joseph, author. | Lerner Publications Company.
Title: Babe Didrikson Zaharias : multisport superstar / Joe Levit.
Description: Minneapolis : Lerner Publications, 2020. | Series: Epic sports bios (Lerner Sports) | Includes bibliographical references and index. | Audience: Ages 7–11 years | Audience: Grades 2–3 | Summary: "Active and tough, Babe Didrikson Zaharias not only broke records, she took athletics by storm, winning two Olympic gold medals for track and field before turning to professional golf. Learn more in this epic biography"— Provided by publisher.
Identifiers: LCCN 2019049869 (print) | LCCN 2019049870 (ebook) | ISBN 9781541597457 (Library Binding) | ISBN 9781728413389 (Paperback) | ISBN 9781728400075 (eBook)
Subjects: LCSH: Zaharias, Babe Didrikson, 1911–1956—Juvenile literature. | Women athletes—United States—Biography—Juvenile literature. | Women track and field athletes—Biography—Juvenile literature. | Women golfers—United States—Biography—Juvenile literature. | Athletes—United States—Biography—Juvenile literature. | Olympics—History—Juvenile literature.
Classification: LCC GV697.Z26 L48 2020 (print) | LCC GV697.Z26 (ebook) | DDC 796.082092 [B]—dc23

LC record available at https://lccn.loc.gov/2019049869
LC ebook record available at https://lccn.loc.gov/2019049870

Manufactured in the United States of America
1-47849-48289-3/9/2020

CONTENTS

THE ONE-WOMAN TEAM

Babe Didrikson arrived at the Amateur Athletic Union (AAU) national track-and-field championships in 1932. She planned to compete by herself against teams from around the United States. Most athletes entered only one or two events for their team. But since Didrikson was competing alone, she entered eight of the 10 events.

Didrikson clears a hurdle while practicing for the national AAU championships.

FACTS AT A GLANCE

Date of birth: June 26, 1911

League: track and field

Professional highlights: won the 1932 AAU national track-and-field championships; won two gold medals and one silver medal at the 1932 Olympic Games; was the first American to win the British Women's Amateur golf tournament

Personal highlights: paid to play on amateur basketball teams in high school; holds two world records for track and field; helped develop the Ladies Professional Golf Association (LPGA)

Once the events started, no one else stood a chance. Didrikson set world records in the baseball throw, the javelin throw, and the 80-meter hurdles. She tied a world record for the high jump, and won the shot put and broad jump.

Didrikson works out at Dyche Stadium in Evanston, Illinois, to prepare for the AAU meet.

Didrikson practices her sprinting.

She scored a total of 30 points and took home the win. The second-place team scored only 22 points—and they had 22 athletes!

NOT YOUR AVERAGE ATHLETE

Mildred "Babe" Didrikson was born on June 26, 1911. From a young age, Babe wanted to compete in physical activities. Boys in her neighborhood wouldn't let most girls play baseball with them. But Babe was different. She played better than most of the boys. Later in life, a reporter asked her if there was anything she didn't play. Babe responded, "Yeah, dolls."

Didrikson was born in Port Arthur, Texas. The area was known for its large oil industry.

Babe even made her chores into fun physical activities. Sometimes she had to clean the large porch that wrapped around two sides of her family's house. Her mother said Babe should get down on her hands and knees to clean the floor. Instead, Babe strapped scrub brushes to her feet, filled the porch with an inch of soapy water, and skated the floor to a fine shine. Other times, Babe would race her older sister Lillie down the street. While Lillie sprinted along the sidewalk, Babe hurdled over the shrubs that divided the lawns between her house and the corner.

Babe took part in several sports in high school. She played baseball, volleyball, golf, and basketball. She spent hours practicing her dribbling, passing, and shooting.

INTO THE HEDGE

When Babe raced against her sister, there was a tall shrub that she couldn't clear. So she asked the owner to trim it. He agreed!

Didrikson (*left*) is shown here wearing an Employers Casualty Company athletic uniform.

The hard work paid off. She made the varsity team her junior year. "I saw possibly twelve thousand young women over those years," Babe's coach said. "I never again saw the likes of her."

Melvin Jackson McCombs was the head coach of one of the best girls' basketball teams in the country. He was so impressed by 15-year-old Babe that he recruited her to work for the Employers Casualty Company, an insurance firm in Dallas, Texas. McCombs offered Babe $75 per month to play for the Golden Cyclones, the company's basketball team, and light office work. Babe and her parents made arrangements with her school. She would leave school and return later for her final exams.

Babe played against the Sun Oil Company her first night in Dallas. The Golden Cyclones won 48–18 with Babe scoring 14 points.

That winter Babe led the Cyclones to the AAU national women's basketball championship game. But the same Sun Oil Company team they'd defeated earlier in the year beat them in the final by one point. Babe was selected as an All-American at her position.

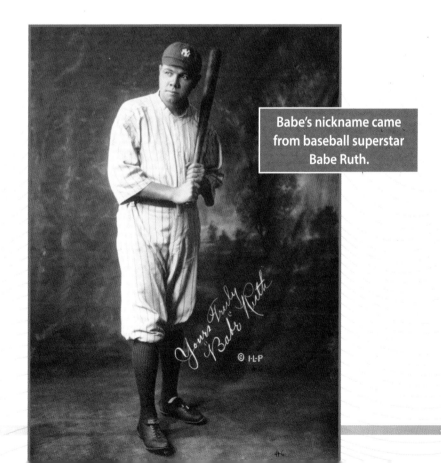

Babe's nickname came from baseball superstar Babe Ruth.

OLYMPIC DREAMS

After Didrikson graduated from high school, Employers Casualty started a women's track-and-field team. They recruited Didrikson immediately. She entered four events in her first meet and won them all. A year later, she won the AAU track-and field championship as a one-woman team.

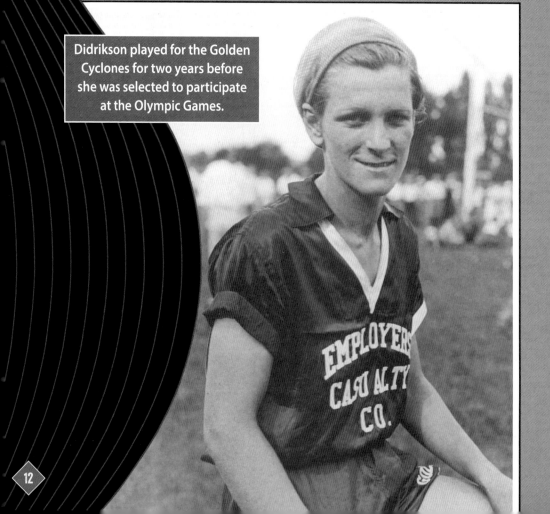

Didrikson played for the Golden Cyclones for two years before she was selected to participate at the Olympic Games.

After the AAU championship, Didrikson was invited to the 1932 Olympic Games in Los Angeles, California. In early July, she left Chicago on a train headed for California. Didrikson jogged up and down the train a few times a day for practice. In her spare time, she annoyed her teammates. She'd yank pillows out from beneath sleeping heads or drop ice cubes down the back of people's dresses.

A SORE WINNER

Didrikson often bragged about her fame. Once she said, "My picture (in the paper) was in the center, blown way up big. There were just little head shots of the others. Man, I just loved that!"

When the train got to Los Angeles, Didrikson made it known that she was there to win. Her teammates were more modest, telling the media they would work hard and hope for the best. Finally, the Games began. Over 100,000 cheering people packed the Los Angeles Coliseum. Female athletes could enter only three events. Didrikson's first event was the javelin throw. She unleashed a mighty toss. It struck the ground 143.3 feet (43.7 m) away, a new world record.

Didrikson demonstrates her javelin technique during practice.

Didrikson (*left*) and Evelyne Hall cross the finish line of the 80-meter hurdles.

Next came the 80-meter hurdles. In the final race, Didrikson and teammate Evelyne Hall burst through the finish line together at 11.7 seconds, breaking the world record. It took the judges half an hour to declare Didrikson the winner. Hall recalls Didrikson yelling, "Well, I won again!"

Didrikson's last event was the high jump. She and teammate Jean Shiley were tied for the gold medal. To break the tie, Didrikson dived over the bar headfirst, a move that was not allowed at the time. Didrikson was forced to take the silver medal.

Didrikson practices the high jump.

Didrikson (*center*) stands on a podium to receive her gold medal for the 80-meter hurdles.

HANDLING CELEBRITY

In March of the following year, Didrikson decided to drive out to California with her mother and sister to secure training with golf pro Stan Kertes.

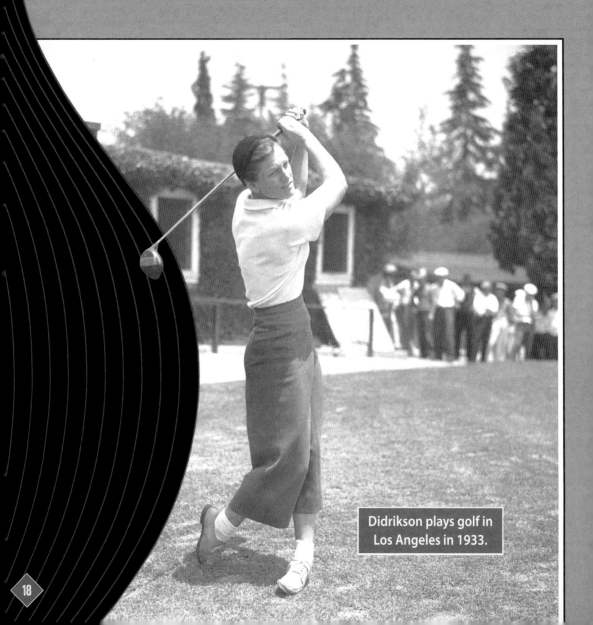

Didrikson plays golf in Los Angeles in 1933.

Didrikson practiced 15 hours a day for six months. "She hit ball after ball until her hands began to bleed, and I had to make her wear gloves and finally beg her to stop and rest," Kertes said. "I knew she had the makings of a champion." And he was right. Didrikson was competitive and willing to put in the work to become a champion.

A DUCK TAKES FLIGHT

Didrikson once played a pro basketball game against the Long Island Ducklings. When her team won, she was given a live duck as a reward. She put the duck in her hotel bathtub overnight. The next day she airmailed it to her parents.

Didrikson returned to Employers Casualty when she got back from golf training. But when her father became ill, she left the company and signed with a sports promoter. She needed to make more money. The promoter organized a barnstorming basketball team: Babe Didrikson's All-Americans. They went on a five-month tour. Didrikson earned $1,000 per month. She sent most of her money home.

Didrikson's barnstorming team included men and women.

After the basketball season, she went barnstorming with a baseball team. She was the only woman on the team. They played more than 200 games across the country that summer. Didrikson was making $1,500 per month—a lot of money at the time. With her earnings, Didrikson bought her father a new car, remodeled her family home, and paid for her sister Lillie's wedding.

FIGHTING TO PLAY

Many people felt sports was an arena for men, not women. A writer for the *New York World-Telegram* said, "It would be much better if [Didrikson] and her ilk stayed home, got themselves prettied up and waited for the phone to ring." Didrikson tried to shake off the hurtful comments. But the constant name-calling started to weigh her down.

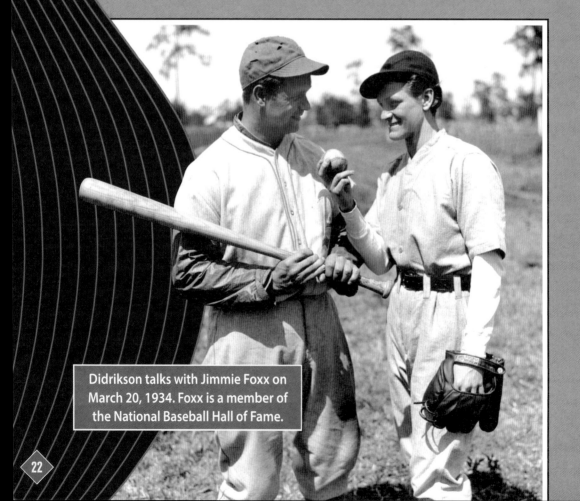

Didrikson talks with Jimmie Foxx on March 20, 1934. Foxx is a member of the National Baseball Hall of Fame.

Didrikson (*left*) stands with Peggy Chandler at the Texas State Women's Amateur Championship.

Didrikson turned wholly to golf in 1934. She signed up to compete in the 1935 Texas State Women's Amateur Championship. Her opponents didn't think Didrikson would fit in with the other women. "We really don't need any truck-drivers' daughters in this tournament," said former state champion Peggy Chandler.

A total of 32 women qualified for the tournament. Didrikson made it to the finals. Her rival was Chandler. They played an exhausting 36 holes: 18 in the morning, 18 in the afternoon. Hundreds of people watched as Didrikson and Chandler took turns leading.

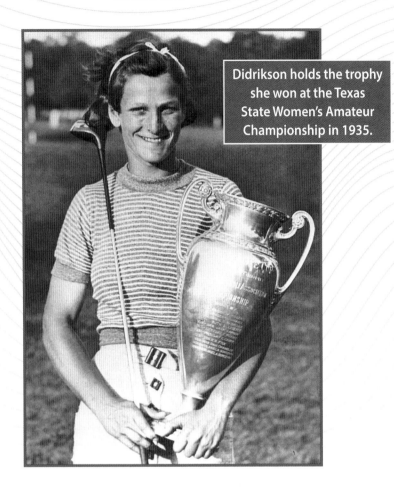

Didrikson holds the trophy she won at the Texas State Women's Amateur Championship in 1935.

On the 33rd hole, Didrikson took the lead for good. She hit one shot from a muddy tire track. The shot helped her win the match and the championship.

After her big win, some people complained to the United States Golf Association (USGA). They said Didrikson was too good to play amateur sports. The USGA agreed, shutting her out of all further amateur tournaments. They said it was in the best interest of the game.

A GOLFING GREAT

The following year, Didrikson was back in California to continue practicing golf. In January 1938, she met professional wrestler George Zaharias. By summer, they announced they were getting married.

Didrikson dances with George Zaharias.

Zaharias entered and won her first major pro golf tournament, the Women's Western Open, in 1944. For more than a year she did not lose a single match. But Zaharias wanted to win the one tournament no American had ever won: the British Women's Amateur. There was just one problem, Zaharias was a pro golfer. Fortunately, her husband made a good living as a businessman and Zaharias was able to take a three-year break from golf, requalifying her for amateur events. Undefeated and strong, Zaharias entered the 1947 British Women's Amateur. Zaharias became the first American to take the trophy.

Zaharias plays in the British Women's Amateur on June 12, 1947.

Zaharias raises her hat in victory after another golf win.

After returning to the United States, Zaharias helped develop a pro golf league for women, the Ladies Professional Golf Association. She became the public face of the group. Zaharias would take home more than 41 titles in the first six years of the LPGA. She played until 1953 when she was diagnosed with colon cancer. She made a brief return to golf in 1954, the month following a major surgery. Zaharias would take home one last title, the Vare Trophy, before her death on September 27, 1956. She was 45 years old.

SIGNIFICANT STATS

Basketball

- averaged 32 points per game in 1931

Golf

- won 14 golf tournaments in a row

Track and Field

- scored 30 points by herself in the 1932 AAU national track-and-field championships

- threw a baseball more than 270 feet (82 m)

- earned two gold medals and one silver medal at the 1932 Olympics

amateur: playing sports without payment

barnstorming: traveling around the country making brief stops to entertain

champion: a winner of the first prize or first place in a competition

hurdles: races in which runners must jump over barriers

meet: a track-and-field competition

promoter: a person who organizes public sports events

rival: a person who competes with another for the same achievement

varsity: a school's top team

SOURCE NOTES

8   Russell Freedman, *Babe Didrikson Zaharias—The Making of a Champion* (New York: Houghton Mifflin Harcourt, 1999), 9.

10   Freedman, 26.

13   Freedman, 40.

15   Freedman, 62.

19   Freedman, 78.

22   "Celebrating Women's History Month: Wonder Girl," Baker Donelson, May 31, 2012, https://www.bakerdonelson.com /Celebrating-Womens-History-Month-Wonder-Girl-05-31-2012.

23   Freedman, *Babe Didrikson Zaharias,* 90.

24   Freedman, 108.

FURTHER INFORMATION

"Babe Didrikson Zaharias: Excellence in Many Forms"
http://www.socialstudiesforkids.com/articles/ushistory
/babezaharias1.htm

Babe Didrikson Zaharias Museum
https://www.trekaroo.com/activities/babe-didrikson-zaharias
-museum-beaumont-texas

Girls Golf
https://www.girlsgolf.org/

Leed, Percy. *Wilma Rudolph: Running for Gold.* Minneapolis: Lerner Publications, 2021.

McCue, Elizabeth McGarr. *Women Athletes Who Rule! The 101 Stars Every Fan Needs to Know.* New York: Liberty Street, 2018.

Scheff, Matt. *The Summer Olympics: World's Best Athletic Competition.* Minneapolis: Lerner Publications, 2021.

INDEX

PHOTO ACKNOWLEDGMENTS

Image credits: Bettmann/Getty Images, pp. 4, 6, 7, 10, 15, 16, 17, 18, 20, 23, 24, 25, 27;
jamesteohart/Shutterstock.com, pp. 5 (track), 28; doel studio/Shutterstock.com, p. 5
(track-and-field typography); Library of Congress (LC-USZ62-4723), p. 8; Library of
Congress (LC-DIG-ppmsca-39089), p. 11; New York Times Co./Archive Photos/Getty
Images, p. 12; Getty Images, p. 14; AP Photo, pp. 21, 22; Popperfoto/Getty Images, p. 26.
Design element throughout: saicle/iStock/Getty Images.

Cover: Bettmann/Getty Images.